D1552384

FAVORITE
CASTLES

of

Germany

From
Bargain Travel Europe

Photography and Text
By
Michael January

Winged Lion Publications

ISBN-13: 978-0692299654
ISBN-10: 0692299653

FAVORITE CASTLES OF
GERMANY

RHEINSTEIN
REICHENSTEIN
MARKSBURG
ELTZ
COCHEM
TWO FRANKENSTEINS
HEIDELBERG
NEUSCHWANSTEIN
HOHENZOLLERN
HORNBURG
SOMMERSDORF
WARTBURG
KRIEBSTEIN
ROCHLITZ
RÖTTELN
SCHÖNBURG
THURANT
TRAUSNITZ

PREFACE

My quest for castles in Europe began in Germany. I was in the country working on a movie project and knew they must have castles, so went on an exploration trip to the romantic Middle-Rhine where I had seen images of castles clinging to the vineyard covered hillsides of the river where legends of the song of the Loreley would draw sailors to their doom on the shoals of the mighty rock. The first castle I visited was Rheinstein. I've been adding to my bucket list ever since, over multiple trips to various corners of the land, learning the complex history of this beautiful country where so much of our legends and heritage derives. My personal ancestry comes in part from Germany where emigrants left the war ravaged land following the European Wars of Succession of the 17th Century and settled in America before our own revolution. The scars of the conflicts of Europe are still evident in the scars and ruins of many of the medieval castles of the countryside.

When exploring the castles of Germany it is helpful learn the distinctions of the language. There are two words that will indicate a castle "Burg" and "Schloss". Burg is the word for the fortified structure of medieval and earlier times and also meant the town within fortified walls where the people would gather for safety from attack by enemies, and the related Burgruine, is the ruins of a castle not rebuilt. Schloss is the word for a palace or manor, built after the age of gunpowder made stone defense walls obsolete. Many of the castles existing today, if not ruins, even if they began as medieval forts were reconstructed in the romantic revival age of the 19th Century. Some were even built new as palaces in the style of the romantic image of the past. Some castles are a combination of old ruins with attached hotels. With its complex historic system of feudal fiefdoms, there are literally thousands of castles in Germany. Here are nineteen of my favorites.

Michael January

CASTLE RHEINSTEIN

Knight's Watch Over the Rhine River

One of the first castles you reach traveling north from Bingen along the western shore of the wandering Middle Rhine is Castle Rheinstein, which sits perched two-hundred and seventy feet above the river, perfect for its original purpose as a customs post to watch over the traffic traversing up and down the river road. The German Holy Roman Emperor Rudolph von Habsburg lived in the castle from 1282 to 1286 to gain control of the trade area from the unruly robber knights of the area, like the family of nearby Castle Reichenstein.

Originally called the "Konigstein" (King's Tower) when the king was in possession of its tower battlements, and later, Fatzberg Castle. Castle Rheinstein (meaning Rhine-stone) was one of the first castles I ever visited in Germany and impressed me with its cliffside perch. Crossing the drawbridge gate and climbing the multiple levels, Rheinstein is like a discovery, rising through towers and halls to the Knight's Hall high in the stone structure. Looking out the upper

residence chamber window to the river far below you get a sense in your bones of what a medieval knight's life must have been like; the romance of chivalry and a lonely watchful vigilance in your great high tower waiting for the attack of your enemies, or to spy a passing caravan due to be taxed. And no quick trips to the corner market for a midnight snack.

The castle fell under the control of the Archbishops of Mainz in the 14th Century, serving as a fiefdom and sometimes residence of the holders of the title. The castle eventually fell into decay in the 1500s, when its purpose faded and was handed to lesser managers who couldn't afford to maintain it. After the annexation of the lower Rhine by Prussia from French control in 1822, the striking ruin came to the attention of Hohenzollern Prince Frederick Wilhelm of Prussia.

Born in Berlin but in command of a military division in Dusseldorf, Frederick, the nephew of King Wilhelm Frederick III, was an art patron who had taken an interest in the romanticized past of the middle-ages and the legends of the Rhine. In 1823, he purchased the old place, as well as some others along the river. He gave it the name Rheinstein for its rocky perch and hired Gothic revival architect Johann Claudius von Lasaulx for the restoration.

Like many of the crumbling old castles along this part of the Rhine, Rheinstein was turned into a second residence and hunting lodge with all the comforts of the late 19th Century. Lasaulx had been the designer of the restoration of the Elector Palace at Koblenz as well as a number of the other Rhine castles, including Burg Reichenstein next door. After a separation from his ill wife, the Rheinstein Castle was the favorite residence of Prince Frederick, and hosted a number of important dignitary visitors, including the Empress Alexandra of Russia, and England's Queen Victoria, who had married into the German aristocracy through her Prince Albert. Frederick, his wife and youngest son are all buried in the castle chapel.

In the neo-gothic restorations of the 19th Century the castle was decorated with stained glass, wood paneling and frescoes. In the living apartments and halls are a collection of art and antique furniture, giving a view into the life of its later royal residents, rather than the medieval austerity of its early existence, with a selection of armor pieces and antlers adorning the walls.

Rheinstein Castle was a possession of the Hohenzollern family up until the mid-1970's when the nearly abandoned ruin was going to be taken over by the Hare Krishnas, but was bought by the German Opera singer Hermann Hecher to preserve its history as a cultural monument. The castle is still managed by the Hecher family.

The castle and its museum are open daily March to November daily from 10:00 am to 6 pm, with the last admission 30 minutes from closing. From November to February on Saturdays and Sundays 10am to 4:30 pm. Romantic Evening Night Tour visits with a torch lit climb to the castle and drinks in the garden are offered from March to November two or three days per month, with advance reservation required. The walk to the castle takes a bit of a steep but brief uphill hike. The Little Wine Prince Restaurant at the castle with views down to the Rhine River is open similar seasonal hours to the castle but opening at 12 noon. For the best photo op, walk behind the castle and follow the path to a little watch tower jutting from the hill.

To reach Burg Rheinstein by car take the autobahn from Frankfurt, Mainz or Mannheim and get off at Bingen. Cross the Bingerbrück and head north along the western shore of the Rhine. There is a small parking lot along the Rhine River road, but can be easily missed if not looking for it. By train or river cruise, get off at Trechtingshausen, about 30 minutes from Frankfurt/Main. The Roessler Line Rhine Cruise stops at the pier just below the castle

CASTLE REICHENSTEIN

Headless Knight
Sleepy Night

Want to take a wine tasting tour of German Rhine wines, a bargain romantic honeymoon hideaway, or darn it, you just like castles where headless apparitions clank down the halls in the dead of night. The Middle Rhine which snakes like a wide ribbon of inland sea lane between Mainz and Cologne is where they keep some of Germany's best kept medieval keeps. There are some 20 or so of the towered, turreted fortresses, some ruins, some preserved, and quaint medieval towns as the river winds lazily toward the North Sea. Around every bend another stone edifice stands watch over the freight barges which motor day and night, up and down the river, past the famous mighty rock called The Loreley where the long golden-haired siren's song of legend drew love-sick lusty, wayward sailors crashing into the rocky shallows.

Each castle has its own story in the long history of Germany's medieval past and Castle Reichenstein which has been featured on an episode of the television series "Ghost Hunters" has one of the more interesting, at least if you believe the legends. Burg Reichenstein is one of the oldest of the Rhine castles, originally built in the early 12th Century. From the mid 13th Century, a family of "robber knights" who owned the castle would prey on errant merchants carrying goods along the river, then retreat to their fortress on the steep hill above. Eventu-

ally defeated in 1282 by a force of their annoyed neighbors and the Habsburg Prince Rudolf who held the next castle down the river, Burg Rheinstein, the father of the clan asked that his 10 sons be spared. Rudolf generously offered that he would spare all of the sons the father could walk past, AFTER his head was cut off. According to legend the robber knight's will was so strong that as he took his first step and his head was lopped off, his headless body's powerful legs strode past nine of his sons before finally toppling to the ground. A version of this story is also accorded to a later 17th Century pirate, but what's a legend if it doesn't get passed around?

Reichenstein is well preserved, with the interior reconstructed in Gothic revival style by Koblenz architect Johann Lasaulx and has a nice collection of medieval armor on display throughout its many floors. The castle also has a small hotel and restaurant within its walls, situated in a former hunter's lodge. The castle is quite popular for weddings f understandable with the romance lore and view of the Rhine valley and there is a beer garden in the summer.

CASTLE MARKSBURG

The Rhine's Original Knight's Castle

Marksburg is the only castle along the Middle Rhine River to have survived essentially intact since its medieval knight past. The other castles along the banks of the Rhine have been destroyed by sieges to some extent through wars, or deliberate demolition, with the ones remaining more ruins rebuilt in the revivalist 19th Century. Because of its position high on a promontory difficult to attack from any side, Castle Marksburg has survived in most of its original form, although with some later additions from 700 years of occupants.

Located above the Rhine town of Braubach, about half-way between Mainz and Koblenz on the east shore of the river, and visible from far away, the castle is reached by a five minute walk from the car parking area or for the more athletically inclined, a 25 minute hike uphill from the center of town and river cruise dock. From mid-April to mid-October a shuttle service in the form of a tourist train runs from the Braubach Old Town up to the castle.

First built in the 13th Century as a holding of the Palatinate, the property passed to the Landgraves of Hesse in the 15th Century, one of the reasons for its survival in the Palatine wars which saw the destruction of castles on the other side of the river. Phillip II of Hesse-Rheinfels built a second residence in town, the Castle Phillipsburg, where the European Castle Institute is now located, with a library of 25,000 volumes on castles of Europe located almost directly below Marksburg.

Marksburg Castle gets its name from the St. Mark's Chapel (Markuskapelle) on the first floor of the chapel tower, which is one of the earliest constructions of the castle. There are four gates approaching the castle, starting with the drawbridge gate, then passing through a 25 meter tunnel fortified with seven guns. Continuing across a wooden bridge which could be withdrawn, there was a pit fall, then a staircase carved in the stone abutment leading to the battery yard, then finally through an iron gate into the inner castle yard.

Once serving as a fortress for enforcing tax levies along the Rhine, like Rheinstein up-river near Bingen, the castle of Marksburg later served as a prison under the Landgraves of Hesse, evidenced by the barred windows. Since the middle-ages prisoners were thrown into the dungeon through the "Angstloch" the Hole of Fear. Today, the German Castle Association maintains a display of medieval torture instruments in the torture chamber cellar. The Gothic Hall has an impressive open fireplace

big enough to walk in. The castle also displays an exhibition of armor and armament over the ages and has a restaurant, the Burgschänke above the drawbridge gate with terrace views. Entrance into the castle is through guided tour only.

BURG ELTZ

Knights Castle of the Mosel Valley

Eltz Castle (Burg Eltz) has one of the most unique profiles of castles, a tall cluster tower of capped turrets, in the form of construction called "Randhausburg", a circular walled fortress residence around a courtyard, and has the distinction of being one of the very few medieval castles in the region west of the Rhine to have not been destroyed in war and to survive in much of its original form, at least since the 14th Century. Visually striking and solitary in its verdant valley near the Mosel River, the castle has often been mentioned as a favorite among travelers and castle lovers.

The Castle of Eltz, dating from the age of the Stauffer kings of the 12th Century has remained in the same family for over 850 years until the present. The first mention of a castle at Eltz was in a deed issued in 1157 by the German Holy Roman Emperor Frederick Barbarossa, witnessed by Rudolf von Eltz. At the time, Rudolf held a small castle next to the Eltzbach, the hillside range of protecting mountains along the north banks of the Mosel River. This was an important trade route from the imperial city of Trier along the river to the fertile farmlands of Maifeld and the road to Koblenz. Parts of the earliest castle, the Romanesque era keep Platt-Eltz and four floors of the living quarters, can still be seen, with one of the oldest painted chimneys in Germany.

17

The Burg Eltz castle is also curious in that it housed three branches of the same family in different sections of the castle. In 1268, three von Eltz brothers had a dispute over inheritance and the family split into three hereditary lines. They divided the estate, but remained in the same fortress, a familial "Ganerbenburg". The castle at that time had fortifying defence walls. The tower keep to the north of the main keep called the "Klein Rodendorf" was built by Theodore zu Eltz between 1290 and 1300 for his family line identified by the heraldic "Buffalo Horns", while not to be outdone, Johann zu Eltz, the son of second brother Wilhelm, built the five stories of the tower called the "Rübenach House" about 1326, for his line of the family "the White Lion".

Then in 1331 came the main dispute which shaped the castle in its present form. The Eltz families formed an alliance with their neighbouring castle lords of the Eltzbach in a confrontation with the Archbishop-Elector of Trier, the Burgundian Balduin (Baldwin) of Luxemburg, the brother of the Emperor Henry VII, who was consolidating his control over the region and the dioceses of Worms and Speyer. In what came to be called the "Eltz Feud", Balduin laid siege to the Eltz Castle, building a fortified attack position on a nearby hillside where he launched stones and catapults at the Eltz fortress, and ultimately an early cannon assault, the first documented cannon fire north of the Alps. The siege lasted for nearly five years, until the Eltz knights finally capitulated in 1336, when the fortification walls were demolished, leaving a fortified residence, with construction and additions continued for another 500 years.

The top stories and the roof of the Rübenach House were added in 1442, with the staircase completed in 1444. The large Rodendorf House was built between 1470 and 1520. The Banner Hall in this part of the castle dates from 1470 with a magnificent late-Gothic vault ceiling, once probably part of a chapel. Four more floors of residence were added above in the 16th Century when Hans Adolf zu Eltz married Katharine von Brandscheid zu Rodendorf in 1563, forming the Eltz-Rodendorf branch, allied with Lor-

raine, France. From this period through the 17th Century, the family reached their greatest influence as Electors of Mainz and Trier as counter-reformation Catholics. Their power lasted until Philipp Karl zu Eltz. Prince Elector of Mainz got caught on the wrong side of a power struggle between the Habsburgs of Austria and the Wittelsbachs of Bavaria for the Imperial Crown in 1742.

The castle was fortunate to escape the damage other castles suffered during the 30 Years War of Palatine Succession, when the Catholic French houses were competing wuth the German Protestants for control of central Europe, a conflict which laid ruin to many of the castles of the Rhine lands. The Eltz Castle was saved due to the influence of a family member, Hans Anton zu Eltz-Üttingen who was serving as a high ranking officer with the French, and had the ancestral castle removed from a list of fortresses to be destroyed, while an impromptu raid by a French scavenger squadron moving through the valley was thwarted by the villagers of nearby Müden, who diverted the soldiers into a field of drying corn and set it ablaze.

A tour of the castle leads through a number of the more impressive rooms. The entrance hall of the Rübenach House was converted into an armory and displays the oldest surviving cannon bolts, thrusting weapons and firearms. The Lower Hall was the living room of the Eltz-Rübenach family. It was built in 1326 and houses the famous masterpiece by Lucas Cranach the Elder of "Madonna with Child and Grapes". The Upper Hall with its wall murals,

intricate Gothic chapel Oriel and colorfully illustrated windows is also called the Bed Chamber, for the large carved four-poster bed. Above the entrance, Count Karl von Eltz made a study for his wife in the 1881 romantic revival period. The murals by E. Knackfuß depict Gothic vines framing portraits of Karl with romanticised medieval images of his sons and daughters.

The Elector's Room is named for the two prince electors (Fürsten) from the house of Eltz, Jakob zu Eltz of Trier (1567-1581) and Philipp Carl zu Eltz of Mainz (1732-1743). Its original furnishings document the stylistic developments during the 17th and 18th century and the Knight's Hall is a late medieval construction of the early 16th century with an original heavy oak ceiling and the heraldic wall frieze, now decorated with suits of armour. The Hunting Room contains hunting trophies, elegant hunting weapons, furniture with fine intarsia and an old embrasure dating from the construction period of the castle. The Countess' Room is also called the Children's Room for the paintings of children and young members of the House of Eltz. The room features one of the oldest surviving painted Renaissance beds in Germany, from around 1520. The Banner Hall from about 1480 with its late Gothic vault ceiling is the most spectacular room in the castle, believed to be a chapel originally, later converted to living and dining room for the Rodendorf line. Before departing the tour exits the 15th century kitchen, one of originally four kitchens in the castle serving the different families.

The Eltz Castle Treasury is separate from the guided tour and comprises an important collection with more than 500 exhibits from eight centuries of the Eltz families' history. The exhibition focuses on artworks by German gold and silver smiths, especially from Augsburg and Nuremberg, precious glass and porcelain ware, jewelry and weapons, some ceremonial.

The castle is open daily from 9:30 am to 5:30 pm, from the last weekend of March to first weekend of November, closed in winter. The guided tours begin every 10 to 15 minutes and take about 35 to 40 minutes. The Treasury can be visited without a guide by showing a valid ticket, open until 6 pm. The exhibits are labelled in German by English translation text is provided in a pamphlet. There are two self-service restaurants in the outer castle, with indoor cozy seating or outdoor terrace. There is parking and a shuttle bus. The castle is reached by road from Münstermaifeld and Wierschem. By cruise boat on the Mosel from Moselkern or Treis-Karden, by foot hike or taxi. A castle bus runs on the weekends.

REICHSBURG CASTLE
COCHEM

Majestic Jewel of the Mosel River Valley

Perhaps one of the most visually impressive castles of Germany, certainly not the largest, oldest or historically important, but upon approach, either along the banks of the Mosel River (Moselle) of western Germany, or from above on the winding road from the A 48, the Reichsburg Imperial Castle's cone roof and spired tower stands above the walls like a jewel in a crown, perched on a steep-sloped hilltop, high above the town of Cochem.

The castle was first built around the year 1,000, as the seat of a Palatine Count Ezzo of Erenfriede. Romanesque era foundations are found around the well showing a fortifying of a fortress around the year 1056, when the core of the central main square keep was built with walls up to 12 feet thick. With Palatine infighting coming to a head in 1151, the Hohenstaufen King Konrad III moved from Boppard on the Rhine and seized Cochem Castle from the feuding palatinate counts, making it an Imperial Castle (Reichsburg) of the region under the Hohenstaufers. In the early 14th Century, the castle came under the Archbishop of Trier, Baldwin (Balduin) of Luxemburg who exercised his will as a Prince Elector on the Mosel region, with the castle undergoing a reconstruction, with heavy walls connecting the town and a chain barrier across the river to control the traffic through the valley.

The original castle was destroyed in the Palatine Wars of Succession in the 17th Century when the soldiers of France's King Louis XIV invaded the Rhine and Mosel region. The castle was occupied by the French in 1688 and set on fire and mined with explosives, blowing up the defensive structures on May 19th, 1689 when much of the town was destroyed as well. The castle was seized again by the French under Napoleon in 1794 for a cannonade position commanding the river below. Following the departure of the French after the defeat of Napoleon, and the region returning to German rule, the castle became the property of the town of Cochem. The castle was a ruin until it was bought in 1868 by a wealthy Berlin businessman who had it completely reconstructed in the neo-Gothic romantic revival fervor of the 19th Century, adding the Gargoyle-like knights in armor bearing arms which watch over the river below from the terrace walls.

Cochem is a beautiful quaint town at the heart of the Mosel River valley surrounded by wine vineyards, famed for the Mosel's flowery Reisling wines, which cling to the steep slopes of dark slate along the river. The narrower Mosel has less barge traffic than the Rhine, left mostly to the cruise boats which make regular stops and departures from Cochem. The Cochem village can get very crowded in the summer months, popular with German and foreign tourists alike. The town doesn't have many large hotels, as it is tucked tight along the riverside, but offers many smaller family owned hotels and bed & breakfast type accommodations. Many house near the tourist center will have signs of guest rooms for rent ("gastezimmer frei"). You can try your luck showing up, but get there early on weekends and check at the tourist office just on the river road in the town center.

The castle offers regular daily tours from March 15 to November 15. The castle also offers a "Knight's Meal" medieval feast with costumed servants and maids, hosted by the Lord of the Manor with a goblet of Mosel wine and entertainment provided by jesters and authentic music ending with a knighting ceremony. The medieval meals last about 4 hours and usually held Fridays and Saturday. Tickets must be booked in advance. The castle can be reached by foot from the Mosel Promenade on a trail up the back from the river or up the Schlosstrasse from the center of town starting at the cathedral. By car you can drive up to the upper town and park near the local Grammar School (Gymnasium).

By car, Cochem is about an hour west from Koblenz (where the Mosel joins the Rhine) or an hour and a half from Trier or Luxemburg to the west, two hours from Cologne or Mainz. If castle hunting in the area there are several others along the Mosel, the most preserved including Burg Eltz about 15 minutes drive, Thurant Castle easily reached by road, and Ehrenburg with its unique stonework defenses. From Cochem you can cross the river and follow narrow roads, about an hour direct to Boppard on the Rhine in the midst the middle Rhine castle area.

NEUSCHWANSTEIN

German King's Fantasy Castle in Bavaria

It is the fantasy castle of childhood dreams and possibly Germany's most famous royal palace. In technical terms, it is not a castle at all, but a "schloss", a 19th Century mansion built in the form of a medieval "burg". Where other castles began as medieval fortresses on hilltops for defensive position, this castle was purely constructed as a residence in a location selected for its beauty and view.

Walt Disney was inspired on a vacation trip to Germany by its spires reaching skyward and tenuous perch on the wooded Alps mountainside to create the centerpiece of his fantasy world of Disneyland, his version of the "Sleeping Beauty Castle" to best represent his entertainment empire. Neuschwanstein Castle (Schloss Neuschwanstein) has nothing to do with that particular story, but rather the fantasy in the mind of a "mad" Bavarian king. Located about an hour southwest from Munich at the foot of the Alps, along the Romantic Road in southern Bavaria, near the town of Fussen and overlooking the village of Schwangau, the Neuschwanstein Castle is a monument to the idealized tales of knights and fair maidens of a lost medieval and chivalric past constructed during the romantic revival of the 1800s. This magnificent architectural dream was built by King Ludwig II, the Wittelsbach ruler of Bavaria from 1864 until 1886, nicknamed "Mad Ludwig" for his whimsical palaces and his eccentricities. His masterpiece palace was an intentional idealized

vision of an old German knight's castle intended as a personal retreat for the reclusive king. But this palace built as a royal private home has little in common with true Teutonic knights castles and was not completed until after Ludwig's death.

The storybook castle was built on the hillside over-looking his father's old palace of Hohenschwangau where young Prince Ludwig spent much of his childhood and intended to overshadow it with a panoramic view of the Bavarian Lechtal and Allgäu Alps. A fan of Wagner, the castle's "Singers Hall" music room was intended to remind of Wagner's medieval knights stories of "Tannhäuser" and "Lohengrin" the "Swan Knight", who King Ludwig identified himself with as a young child, operatic odes to lofty gods and the romance of knights' chivalry. Hitler as well was enthralled by the same fantasy idylls of Germany's Teutonic ancestral heritage and held performances of Wagner's operas here, but of course his dream had a whole new meaning.

Neuschwanstein is located near the Forggensee and the town of Fussen on the Austrian border, a stop on the Romantic Road in the Allgäu Alps, and a short distance from Oberammergau and Garmish-Partenkirchen. Schloss Neuschwanstein can be reached off the A95 autobahn about an hour drive from Munich or about 30 minutes from Friedrichshafen. The Schwangau region is a storybook landscape of castles, mountains and lakes with a variety of hiking trails and cycle paths that wind through lush meadows and dark woods. A beautiful drive with a rental car through thick wooded groves past gingerbread alpine houses and lodg-

ings. To get to the entrance of Neuschanstein requires a bit of hiking or a bus ride. Car parking is at the bottom of the hill in the village of Hohenschwangau. It's a 30 minute trek up the hill on foot so plan some time and comfortable shoes. A bus runs from near the ticket box office to the trail near the Marienbrücke bridge. For a few euros extra you can take a horse drawn cart ride to the top. For a photo op take the path beyond the castle to the breathtaking Marienbrücke walking bridge over the Pöllat Gorge. And it is from this side that the best views of the castle can be had, though most of the spectactular photographs you see of the spired castle are from higher up the mountains.

Neuschwanstein os one of the most visited tourist sights in Germany and is nearly always busy. The tour of Neuschwanstein is guided in small groups with timed tickets. If you don't want to drive from Munich, there are daily bus tours available for day trips to Neuschwanstein and Ludwig's other dream palaces like Linderhof nearby, often combined into one tour. Tickets for Neuschwanstein can be combined with Hohenswangau Palace and a recent addition, the Museum of the Bavarian Kings, with the story of the royal Wittelsbachs near the edge of the lake.

TWO FRANKENSTEINS

Mary Shelley's Inspiration

The name of Frankenstein is as fixed in the fascination of the mind with monsters and castles as the end of the creature of Mary Wollstonecraft Shelley's story at the end of her groundbreaking novel. The connection of the literary legend of the Frankenstein story to a castle in Germany, however comes mostly from the Hollywood movie version of the story from the Universal fright factory when Boris Karloff grunted and stalked the stone halls of a castle ruin movie set in 1931. There is no castle really in the book of "Frankenstein: Or The Modern Prometheus" and Mary Shelley never tells where the name came from. But for travelers through Germany with a desire to find castles related to the famous name will lead to two intriguing stories surrounding ruined fortresses.

One of the most enduring monsters of literature and movies was created by Mary Wollstonecraft Shelley, then still Mary Godwin, after one stormy night in Geneva, Switzerland when she and future husband, Percy Bysshe Shelley, along with England's romantic poet-hedonist Lord Byron and his doctor John Polidori, while sitting around the fireplace during a gloomy weather summer in 1816, bet one another they could write scary stories better

that the purveyors of cheap scary pulp literature of the day known as "Penny Dreadfuls". Byron started a vampire story, naming his villain after the fellow who cut down trees at his ancestral Nottinghamshire home, Newstead Abbey, but grew quickly bored. Polidori later finished and published the story as "The Vampyre" with the villain modeled ad mush after Byron himself. Percy Shelley scribbled some middling haunting verse. But the 19 year old Mary, who had never had a novel published before, invented Victor Frankenstein - a student of science so infected by the power of knowledge, made a man from the parts of the dead, only to have the result of his over-reaching ego and hubris destroy him and those he loved. Inspired by the social arguments between Byron and Shelley, and a nightmare "dream" possibly influenced by the experiments of Luigi Galvani who had recently stimulated dead muscle tissue with electricity, and her young romantic trysts with the married Percy Shelly in the graveyard of St. Pancras Parish Church where her mother was buried in London, Mary Godwin created one of the enduring works of gothic literature.

The novel of Frankenstein sets the protagonist of that name coming from Switzerland, inspired by her surroundings in Geneva when she began the story and had him studying at the University at Ingolstadt near Munich in Bavaria. Ingolstadt was one of the first centers of learning in old Germany. The monster actually had no name, but became synonymous with the name of his creator, Frankenstein. Speculation has long resulted in a search for a connection between the name and a real place.

Although a later publishing of the book famously told a version of the genesis of the story, nothing was said of the origin of the name. One suggestion has been made that she might have heard the name from her step-mother, Mary Jane Claire-mont Godwin, who had translated German literature, but Mary pretty much hated her step-mother, who had tried to stop her elopement with Shelly, chasing them all the way to Paris, so it doesn't seem likely she would name her most important work from a suggestion by her step-mother.

The other possibility is that she encountered the name during a trip on the Rhine River in 1814, the year before that fateful Genevan summer with the literary wager. Young Mary Godwin and Percy Shelly had traveled through Europe after their eloping from London to Paris, then traveling through France, Switzerland and returning home to England by boat down the Rhine, and may have visited one of two castles, or heard legends of them along the journey from fellow passengers, most especially three stu-

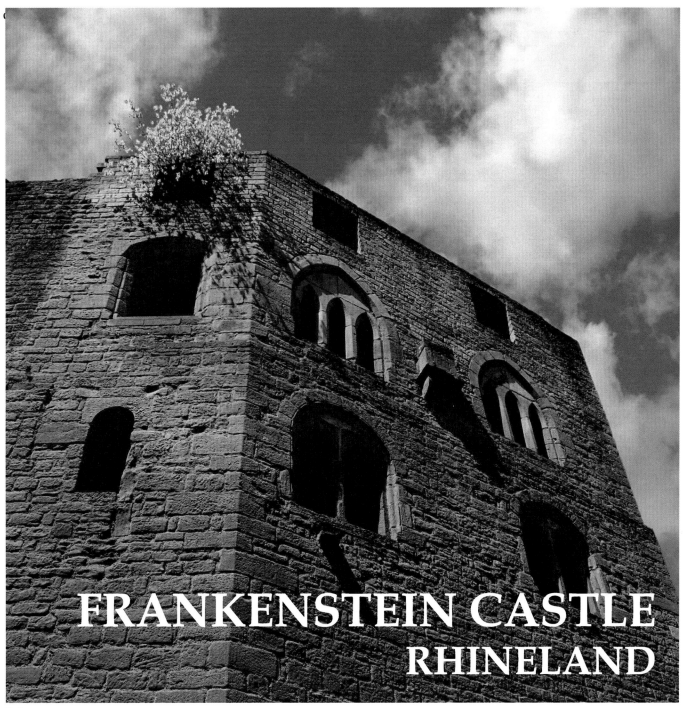

FRANKENSTEIN CASTLE
RHINELAND

Grab Your Pitchfork on the German Wine Road

Along a beautiful winding road in the Rhineland-Palatine region between Kaiserslautern and Mannheim, near the military bases of Ramstein and Landstuhl, familiar to American service personal and just down the road from the wine town of Bad Dürkheim with its annual sausage and wine festival and giant wine barrel, a castle ruin of red limestone stands ominously above a tiny little village with the name of Frankenstein. The castle of Frankenstein of the Rhineland-Palatine was first built at the beginning of the 12th Century, about the year 1100 and expanded in the 14th and 15th Centuries. It was controlled by the Bishops of Speyer and for a time the Monastery at Limburg. From the castle's now tree and vine shrouded ruin walls, one can see the value of the position over the valley with a 190 degree view of the road and town below, and rather unique for a castle, the main railway line to Kaiserslautern which now runs through a tunnel right under the ruins.

This Burg Frankenstein castle has a fairly sketchy history and is not even marked on some maps, suggestive of hidden secrets? There is no admission or visitor center here, just a marked trail past the village cemetery. Visitors can park at the rail crossing and hike up a steep path up to the ruins and along a nature trail through the hills. The ruin encompasses a

few remaining walls where the former main hall stood. Suffering the ravages of time and struggles for control of the region, the castle at Frankenstein was occupied by the Spanish and the French in various wars and suffered much of its destruction during the Thirty Years War of European Succession.

Strikingly, upon view of the Castle Frankenstein ruins, clinging to a rock over-looking the small town with the infamous name, one can picture the angry villagers with pitchforks storming the castle while Boris Karloff rages from the burning battlements. And if peering close, one can almost see the face of the monster in the rocky crag to which the castle ruins cling, which might have inspired a young woman author surrounded by men of notoriously monstrous talent and egos.

As for other castles with the name Frankenstein, which roughly interprets as "fortress of the Franks", refering to the early medieval rulers who held sway in central French and German speaking Europe, there is a castle overlooking the Rhine River, Burg Gutenfels, that some tour operators

refer to as Frankenstein (it fits better on the boat tour) but was actually built by the von Falkensteins, so is really a Falkenstein castle, but easily confused for non-German speakers, and the castle which is more commonly suggested as inspiration of the horror book name, the ruin in Darmstadt near Frankfurt with legends of a doctor amd alchemist who experimented with the dead. The castle of the Rhineland wine country is the more visually dramatic of the two Frankensteins, but in the end, the 19 year old authoress of the world's most famous monster may not have set foot in any castle named Frankenstein, but legends grow in mysterious ways.

FRANKENSTEIN CASTLE
DARMSTADT

Where Literature, Legend and Halloween Meet

The legend of a monster and mystery of creation meet near the town of Darmstadt, about half an hour from Frankfurt in the Hesse region of Germany. Fifteen minutes south of the city and the airport and just off the A5 autobahn, a winding road takes you up a mountain to the ruins of a castle called Frankenstein. An original fortress was first built with a view of the flat Rhine valley in the 10th Century. The current castle was constructed beginning in the 13th Century with additions in the next two hundred years. Abandoned as a residence in the late 1600s, and serving for a while as a prison and then completely forgotten, the castle has been a ruin ever since, with just a few remaining walls, an intact though damaged distinctive high observation tower, and a small chapel, said to be haunted. While the name of the Frankenstein castle of Darmstadt was resurrected in romantic age of the 1800s as a result of the era's fascination with gothic and romantic literature spurred by the publishing of Mary Shelley's famous novel of "Frankenstein" in 1818, the structure itself was never rebuilt like some others and remains just a shadow of a former fortress. The inspiration for the haunting famous novel of Gothic horror has been the subject of speculation ever since its first printing and attempts to connect the name with an actual place have been tantalizing, though never proven.

Uncovering Mary Shelley's inspiration is more complex. In the novel, Victor von Frankenstein is not German at all but Swiss from Geneva. Her story was most famously begun at Lake Geneva in the summer of 1816. The science student's decidedly under-detailed creation of an unnamed "creature" were carried out at Ingolstadt University and most of the story takes place in Switzerland, the Alps, and on a ship in the frozen Arctic. There is a suggestion that Mary Shelley visited the Darmstadt Frankenstein ruin on a boat trip down the Rhine River in 1814. There is no record of a visit to Darmstadt, or mention of it in her journals. She perhaps may have heard of it from Byron, who spent more time in Germany than the Shelleys, and wrote of his journeys in his seminal work "Childe Harold". Bryon may have heard stories of the castle and its legend of a physician, crackpot theologian

and alchemist, Johann Dippel, who was rumored to have tried to raise the dead by experimenting with human corpses during in the castle's days as a prison. Dippel was trying to discover the alchemist's "Elixer Vitae" potion of eternal life from blood and body fluids. He supposedly got the Landgrave of Hesse to grant him possession of the castle, which had once belonged to a family Franckenstein, in exchange for the life extending formula, but instead what he created was foul-smelling concoction known as "Dippel's Oil" made from animal bones, better suited to cloth dies and sheep dip than creating eternal life. The only very tenuous connection to be made from the Frankenstein novel to Dippel's nefarious doings might be found in an offhand joke made to a pregnant Mary Shelley while she was working on the book, taking a remedy of

mixed Aniseed Spirit and a whale fat called Spermaceti, to which Percy Shelley quipped might be added "9 drops of human blood, 7 grains of gunpowder, 1/2 ounce of putrified brain and 13 mashed grave worms", perhaps a reference to local villager jokes about what Johann Dippel was up to.

A suggestion for the Frankenstein name has also been assigned to Mary's step-mother Mary Clairmont, who may have had contact with Jacob Grimm for William Godwin's children's book publishing venture in London. Darmstadt is not far from Hanau, the birthplace of the fairy tale writing brothers and the start of the Fairy Tale Road from Hanau to Bremen. Though, that's even less likely as Mary Shelley's relationship with her step-mother was not good and they where not on speaking terms. The early 1800s was a time when the mysteries of science and medicine were meeting the mysteries of life. A panic of being buried alive had caused coffins of the time to be made with bells on a rope that could be rung if the mistakenly buried came back to life. Mary Godwin, later taking the name of her mother, Wollstonecraft, and her husband, Shelley, had also heard from her father's friends, Charles Lamb and Samuel Taylor Coleridge, stories of experiments at Newgate prison of electricity being passed through dead prisoners, and the experiments of Luigi Galvani making frogs legs twitch with electric jolts. The idea of corpses surging to life in "Galvanism" perhaps excited the imagination in Mary's formative teen years. The invention of her story "in a dream" had come after the reading of a German collection of horror stories called the

"Fantasmagoriana" that famous summer night in 1816 on the shores of Lake Geneva. The novel of Frankenstein and what inspired it is as much a collection of inspirations as her monster is of collected bits of dead bodies.

The Castle Ruins of Burg Frankenstein in Darmstadt have been popularized by its name over the years and by its proximity to a military base, serving as the end of a run to the top of the hill from Cambrai-Fritsch Kaserne Army Base. It was mostly American soldiers who brought the idea of Halloween as a holiday party to Germany and the castle with the scary name seemed the perfect place. The Darmstadt Frankenstein Castle has become the location for one of the largest Halloween scare-show celebrations in the country, with spook effects and music, food and drink partying over three weekends at the end of October and November.

The Ruins of Burg Frankenstein can be reached by car off route B426 to a parking lot down the hill or by public transportation on the "Frankenstein Bus" from Darmstadt during the Halloween weekends and to the bus stop the rest of the year, but the walk from the bus stop is indeed a hike. The road and slope up the hill to the castle is a popular destination for bike riders and runners. There is a restaurant at the castle which hosts weddings and other events with beautiful views of the valley. The ruins have become quite popular in the "Goth" world with photographers taking pictures of glam girls in black dresses freely haunting its stone walls.

HEIDELBERG CASTLE

Germany's Most Famous "Beautiful Ruin"

A poet once gave a definition of beauty as "the blue sky and clouds showing through the windows of the ruins of Heidelberg Castle." The combination of the red stone and gothic arched filigree of the old destroyed hall against a cloud filled sky of blue embraced by the green trees of the Konigstuhl mountainside where it stands overlooking the old town of Heidelberg and the Neckar River has been a fascination for tourists for over two centuries. Heidelberg is undoubtedly Germany's best known romantic city, a reputation due principally to its castle and its lovely old town below. Since tourism became a pre-occupation of the wealthy and the literati in the

early 19th Century, Heidelberg's castle has been one of the most painted, revered and commented on castle ruins in Germany's Rhineland and one of its most visited.

The castle has a complex history, home to the Electors of the German Palatine, destroyed and rebuilt, hit by lightning, set a blaze, and bombarded by cannon shells. Mark Twain who wrote of the castle ruin at Heidelberg in his "A Tramp

Abroad", eloquently describing the ruin of its "Fat Tower", split in half by the explosion of a powder magazine when French solders set the castle on fire in 1633, once commented that the French made the most beautiful ruins, for the destruction of many of the castles in the south-western part of Germany, but it was the Swedish Army who defeated the castle in the 30 Years War, by maneuvering cannons to positions on the hill above. The castle suffered even more destruction at the hands of the residents of Heidelberg who would mine its stones to build houses. And it was a Frenchman who came to the castle's rescue when Heidelberg came under the control of Baden and plans for its demolition were proposed, but Count Charles de Graimberg instead promoted it as a tourist destination.

The remaining main halls of the castle forming its most recognizable façade date from the Renaissance. The geometric castle terraces form even levels for strolling among its ruins as Victor Hugo once did. In the south-east end of the gardens one can find what remains of the "Great Grotto" which once had trick water fountains like those at Salzburg's Hellbrunn, but now gone. Johann Goethe was also a fan of the castle and a plaque dedicated to him is still to be found on the wall of the former aviary, still a target of birds no longer captive. The King's Hall (Königsaal) now used for events, banquets, weddings and concerts, wasn't added until the early 20th Century. During the Heidelberg Castle Festival in the summer, the courtyard is the location of open air musicals, operas and theatre performances and concerts performed by the Heidelberg City Orchestra, like the classic "Castle Serenades".

One of the castle's best known attractions is the giant wine barrel, which has appeared in fantastic fiction and history, referenced in the writing of Jules Verne, Victor Hugo and Mark Twain, and even that notorious fictional teller of outsized tales, Baron Münchausen. In the days of the royal princes, the Palatine taxes were often paid in goods rather than gold and the wine growing vineyards which line the valleys of the Neckar River and the Rhineland produced lots of wine, so each year, a portion of the crop was due to the prince. There have been a few barrels under the foundations of the castle of Heidelberg but the present Heidelberg Tun, sometimes called the "largest wine barrel in the world" was built in 1751 by the Prince Elector Karl Theodor. It is 23 feet high and 27 feet wide capable of holding 55,000 gallons of wine, though it has been dry for a few centuries and reportedly took 30 oak trees to construct.

Heidelberg's wine barrel is associated with the legend of Perkeo whose colorful image can be seen perched on the wall across from it, forever on guard and adorning the signs of a number of drinking establishments in the old city as the unofficial mascot of the region. Perkeo was a dwarf from the Austrian-Italian Tyrol brought by Prince Karl Phillip to Heidelberg in 1720 to serve as court jester. His common nickname reportedly came from his answering "why not" in Italian whenever asked if he'd like another glass of wine. He was given mastery of the castle wine stocks and lived to a ripe old age of 80, legendarily only drinking wine, until he became ill. A doctor gave him a glass of water to drink and he died the following day.

The wine barrel is cramped into the stone foundations of the castle, climbed by wooden ladders to the top, which has been used as a dance floor upon occasion. There are ax marks on the dark wooden staves, supposedly from the French soldiers who occupied Heidelberg, expecting to slake their thirst only to find it empty. Step outside the castle to the terrace overlooking the city below, on the west corner of the castle look for the gargoyle head in the shape of a lion. In other castles these openings were used for defense, pouring boiling oil or water, but at Heidelberg it is actually an overflow outlet from the wine barrel inside.

Also at the Heidelberg Castle is the German Pharmacy Museum (Deutsches Apothekenmuseum) with the entrance off the courtyard in the catacomb basements of the Ottheinrichsbau. The museum houses a collection of over 20,000 objects presenting a journey through the history of medical science, especially focused on the development of pharmacology as first nearly a magic art, then a science. The collection on display is one of the largest in the world, covering two thousand years of western

pharmacy history. Remedies for illness had been practiced since the dawn of man, but the official recognition of the pharmacist came in 1231 when the German Emperor Frederick II registered the first regulation of the practice with laws laying out the rights and the duties of physicians and pharmacists. A self-guided tour leads through several recreated rooms, featuring aspects of the development of cures from herbs and the Alchemist's art, to the modern drug lab. 16th Century Physician Theophrastus von Hohenheim, who called himself Paracelsus, practiced the development of pharmaceutical alchemy. While alchemists originated by trying to turn base metals into gold, Paracelsus's vision was the formation of effective medicinal remedies from the combining of elements. The chemist's shop of the 19th Century is represented by the premises of the "Crown Pharmacy" of J. Faulhaber which once stood on a corner in the city of Ulm.

The castle can be reached on foot from the old town of Heidelberg, but a Bergbahn (mountain train) funicular to the top of the Konigstuhl mountain stops at the castle. The funicular station is in the parking structure #2 at the Kornmarkt stop of bus 33, or on foot just a block behind the old town hall and main square. There is a restaurant and beer and wine hall located at the castle, operated by Mövenpick. For more castles less famous, with a car you can head east from Heidelberg along the Neckar River and the along castle road.

HORNBURG CASTLE
HOTEL & RESTAURANT

German Knight's Castle of the Neckar Valley

The Neckar River flows northward from industrial Stuttgart through Heilbronn where it winds lazily through the Odenwald Forest and the Neckar Valley (Neckartal) of hillslopes lined with wine grape vineyards and castles to Heidelberg, then onward through Mannheim to meet up with the mighty Rhine. Germany's "Castle Road" follows the river through this part of Baden-Württemberg from Heidelberg to Heilbronn where the idyllic mountain hills evoke a lost time and quiet romance.

Standing above a wide curve of the river the tower of Burg Hornberg stands sentinel over the barges which through the river locks below. This 11th Century castle was once the home of a German knight of curious legend, with a modern connection to Japan and comic books. The knight Götz von Berlichingen lost one of his hands in a tournament and had it replaced with an artificial iron glove. It is suggested that the German knight Götz is the inspiration for

the hero "Guts" of the popular Japanese Manga graphic novel series "Berzerk" and he indeed was the inspiration of the first play by written by Goethe. Legend or not, the grandson of Götz von Berlichingen sold the castle after his death to the Barons of Gemmingen who have owned it for twelve generations. Since 1953 the Gemmingens have operated a hotel and restaurant at this unique castle in a former stable. The main castle is for the most part a magnificent ruin with its original tower still intact, sitting atop a steep-sloped mountain, surrounded by grape vineyards on the riverside and dark forest on the other. The castle is easily reached by car, driving through the medieval stone gate into the courtyard, but parking can be tight if the restaurant is busy with locals.

The hotel portion of the Burg Hornberg takes up two floors in a cozy stone and wood beam building. The rooms are more like a country inn, but with a warm lounge including a suit of armor on watch, private balconies look out into the deep wooded forest slope behind, and just steps across the medieval courtyard from the restaurant. The Burg Hornberg restaurant, which began in the stable of the castle, expanded with windows and an open air terrace looking out on a spectacularly romantic view of the Neckar Valley, offers a selective gourmet dining menu taking inspiration from regional dishes of Swabia and Baden, along with a selection of wines, including vintages from the castle's own vineyards.

The current Baron von Gemmingen runs the castle hotel and restaurant with personal attention, bringing his experience of managing major resort hotels home to the family business. The Hornberg Castle makes for a romantic stop on a Neckar Valley wine tasting tour and a central base for country and forest walks, biking, exploring the other castles and medieval towns of the Neckar Valley, Mosbach, Bad Wimpfen and Rothenberg where the "Castle Road" meets the "Romantic Road". The Technical Museum at Sinsheim is about 45 minutes away and Heidelberg is about an hour to the west along the winding road which follows the river bank through steep slopes. The other castle in the von Gemmingen family, Guttenberg Castle, is visible across the valley and a short drive across the river.

The Hornberg Castle and Restaurant are a popular location for romantic castle weddings (in its authentic gothic chapel), receptions and wine tasting tours with the spirit of Götz von Berlichingen not far away, watching over the modern day guests to his medieval knights castle, as one of his iron gloves (a replica) hangs on the restaurant wall next to his portrait.

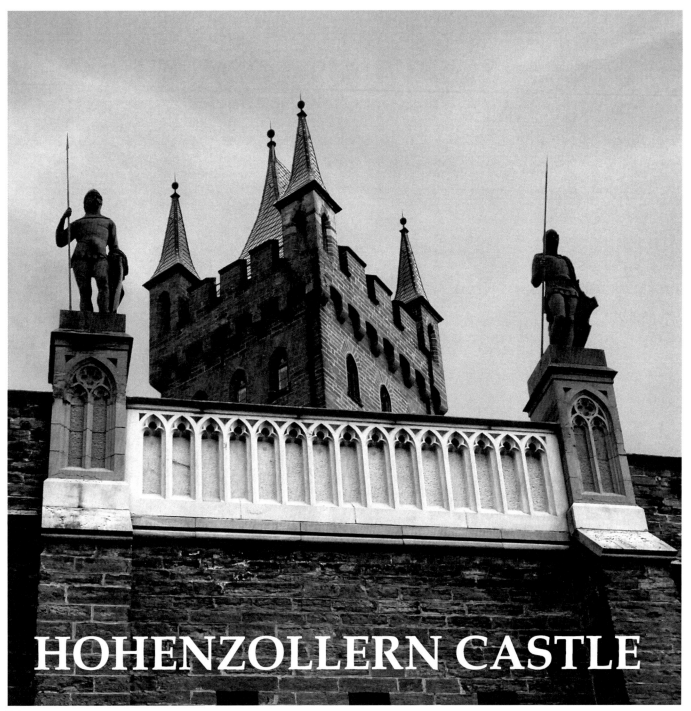

HOHENZOLLERN CASTLE

Black Forest
Palace in the Clouds

Swabia, Germany is the region in the southwest, between the Black Forest and Bavaria along the Upper Danube River which flows eastward through southern Germany toward Hungary. The Hohenzollern family is one of the great dynasties of Europe, originally from Prussia, once ruling over portions of Swabia, Bavaria, Franconia and Prussia in Germany and connected by marriages and complicated lineages to the British and Russian Royal families with the culmination of Kaiser Wilhelm II, Germany's last Emperor before the modern era, since WWI tended to level monarchies into the dustbin of history.

The ancestral castle of the Hohenzollern, sits high on a mountaintop "the Zoller hill" overlooking the Danube (Donau) Valley at the eastern edge of the Black Forest, sometimes shrouded in clouds like a legendary mythical fairytale castle. The original fortress of the 11th Century was destroyed in the 15th Century. It was rebuilt and expanded in the 17th Century in its current footprint, with most of the early form of the

medieval period stripped away or redesigned, and rebuilt virtaully from the ground up, but fell to disuse when the family moved to the more easily reached palace castle in nearby Sigmaringen. In the early 19th Century, the castle became a reconstruction project for the imperial family history enthusiast, Crown Prince Frederick, also responsible for a number of Rhine castle revivals, and recreated in the neo-gothic style, completed in 1867, mostly as a ceremonial showplace.

Aside from a majestic castle outline on its mountaintop, often appearing like an island in the sky above the clouds, one of the curious and unique features of this grand landmark is the complex royal family genealogy which Kaiser Wilhelm II wallpapered onto the grand entry way, the "Ancestral Hall" to illustrate the royal family tree. Rare among castles is the circular driveway to the Eagle Gate, obviously built for carriages of the 19th Century, almost rather like a modern parking structure to overcome the steep mountain approach to the castle. Grand rooms and parlors fitting a royal palace, secret medieval underground passageways only discovered in 2001, now display family china and gold dishware and two coffins which once held the remains of Frederick the Great and his son. And for more morbid curiosity, resting on a hallway table are two death mask molds of a couple members of the family.

The Hohenzollern castle also holds the Royal Treasury of the Hohenzollerns. The treasure was divided in a property dispute in the 1920s, but the magnificent Royal Prussian Crown, actually a replacement for an earlier original sold off piecemeal, can be seen in a safe in the former castle kitchens turned into the treasury room. There is an armor collection, but no comparison to that in the other Hohenzollern family castle at Sigmaringen. On the

terrace below the walls to the southwest are several statues of the later members of the great family, emperors in outsized proportion, gazing out over the land.

The Hohenzollern Castle at Hechingen in Baden-Wurttemburg is about an hour south of Stuttgart and one and a half hours from Munich. The castle rooms are only seen by group tours. The grounds and secret tunnels can be explored as well. The hiking path up the hill is quite steep and long. There is a restaurant "Burgschenke", below the castle.

SOMMERSDORF CASTLE

Moats and Mummies on the Romantic Road

It was like a scene from a Gothic romance novel of knights errant and the chivalric days of yore. A wandering poet-knight on a quest happens on a small but majestic castle, caught in the last fading sun's rays and the cool shades of eve, the cobalt dusk sky reflecting on the still waters of the wide moat. Crickets prattled in the fresh mown hay and the bull frogs sang their throaty baritone songs of love. The great gate across the moat bridge had been closed and secured, yet the visitor knocked with hope of hospitality. The entreaty was answered by the lord of the castle and sanctuary granted in the very chamber above the castellans own private chambers for a respite from the hardships of travel. A night spent in the ancient wood-beamed heart of the romantic fortress was rewarded with a breakfast served in the morning prepared by the very lady of the castle. Ah, this is no fable of fantasy but a real castle where you can stay on your own romantic poet's journey. And this was pretty much what happened to me, on my visit.

Schloss Sommersdorf in the region of Germany known as Franconia in northern Bavaria, near where the Romantic Road and the Castle Road cross, seems a world away and lost in time. The Sommersdorf Castle has been in the von Crailsheim family since 1550, when Wolf von Crailsheim brought Protestantism to the neighborhood, though the castle's origins date back to 1208. The moat and walls still encircle the castle which comprises the Old Castle, watch tower, church and the New Castle added in 1750. Schloss Sommersdorf is not a full service

castle hotel, rather a lived in private home which offers bed & breakfast lodging in two guest rooms and three furnished self-catering apartments in the old castle and a former granary, with their own common rooms for games, television and privacy, making for a truly unique and mythical medieval castle stay. You won't find any conference center or meeting rooms at Schloss Sommersdorf, just peace and quiet in the countryside. Two rooms are within the main castle including the atmospheric Gothic Room on the floor above the owner's own private home apartments.

The Crailsheims are a large extended family dynasty with a tradition of public service and still own several castles. One von Crailsheim was a high official in the court of King Ludwig II and was the one who tried to have him certified insane for his incessant castle building. The current resident of Schloss Sommersdorf, located in the tiny village of Sommersdorf, a few miles from the A6 autobahn south of Ansbach, Baron Manfred Dr. von Crailsheim, retired from his office in nearby Dinkelsbühl to enjoy his classic cars and maintain the family property with his wife. If staying at Schloss Sommersdorf the good doctor will proudly show you his 1905 Cadillac and 1913 Ford "Tin Lizzie". He'll even take you for a tour around the beautiful back roads of the Franconia hills. And if you press him you might even get a peek at the family mummies!

Okay, back to the mummies in a moment… Franconia essentially means the lands of the Franks, the tribe which arose during the 5th Century from the crumbling of the Roman Empire. The most famous of the Franks was Charlemagne, (Karl der Grosse for the Germans) the first Holy Roman Emperor. Charlemagne's empire was divided into three parts. The easternmost became Germany and the western became France, while those two have been fighting over the middle part ever since, with the last time in World War II.

Relatively rural and sparsely populated, the lands of Franconia are noted for many of the remaining walled cities of Germany and castles which now make up the tourism trails of castle routes and romantic era, like Rothenburg ob der Tauber, Dinkelsbuhl and Nuremberg. The little village of Feuchtwangen (meaning "Wet Cheeks") a kilometer away, is legendarily where Charlemagne got lost and stopped to splash water on his face. Franconia also saw a lot of troop movements of Napoleon. It was Napoleon who ceded parts of Franconia to his ally Bavaria.

It was while Napoleon's troops stopped at Sommersdorf in 1806, that they discovered five coffins in the family crypt under the castle's church. The coffins contained well-preserved mummified remains, four of them family members, and one a Swedish army colonel, Baron von Holz, from the Thirty Years War, found still wearing his boots. One of the mummies was buried alive, the Baroness von Kniestett, who became ill after the birth of a child and thought

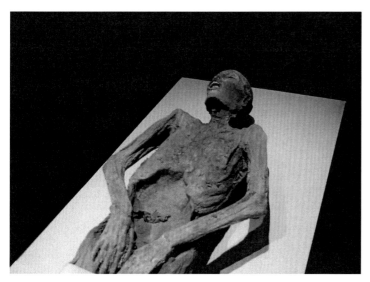

to have died, but the clenched fingers of her mummified corpse show that she was buried too soon. Why the mummies were naturally preserved is still an unsolved mystery. To preserve them from deterioration, the coffins are no longer opened for casual inspection, but the good baron will take you into the crypt for a look at the coffins, which remain were they have rested for 300 years, although they may go out for a tour of museums on occasion.

A stay at Schloss Sommersdorf offers an opportunity for lots to explore. Passing just outside of Sommersdorf is the former Roman boundary known as the Limes (Limit). Within easy reach are colorful medieval towns of the Romantic Road, the Neckartal valley, the Altmuhltal Nature Park, the city of Ansbach a few miles to the north with its connection to the American Revolution Battle of Yorktown, and the great walled city of Nuremburg. The nearby town of Wolframs-Eschenbach, was once a stronghold of the Teutonic Knights, named for Germany's epic poet Wolfram von Eschenbach, author of the legend of "Parsifal" one of the Minnesänger minstrel poets who roamed medieval Franconia with their songs of love and chivalry, who was born there and is buried in the town church.

R eservations for Schloss Sommersdorf can be made by query through the website Schloss-Sommersdorf.de. There is a minimum three night stay. Schloss Sommersdorf is just under two hours from Munich or Frankfurt by car. The nearest rail station is Triesdorf-Merkendorf about 4 miles away, a little over two hours from Munich, but public transportation is limited to local rural bus service. But that's why you come to Middle Franconia isn't it, to get away off-the-beaten track.

WARTBURG CASTLE

Martin Luther, His Bible, His Devil and a Saint

Leave a man alone in his room with a pen and inkwell and he can change the world. After his refusal to recant his views in opposition to the Catholic Church's selling of indulgences at the Diet of Worms in 1521, Martin Luther hid out at Wartburg Castle in the Thuringian forest town of Eisenach. Luther had lived briefly in the town of Eisenach under his own name, but while staying in a lonely small room at the end of the guard's walk at Wartburg Castle, the exiled former monk hid out under the name of "Junker Jörg" (The Knight George). He spent his time translating the Latin bible into German, creating the "Luther Bible". The translation, suggested by his friend Melanchthon took eleven weeks to complete, finished after he had left the castle confines.

It seems that the stay was a rough time for Luther, fighting the inner demons of depression, while outwardly fighting the Devil. The Lutherstube (Luther's Room) at Wartburg castle no longer contains the original furniture when Luther was there, except for a curious whale bone stool, but has been recreated. The one piece not replaceable was the famous ink stain on the wall where Luther was said to have flung his inkwell at the devil. He apparently missed because the devil is surely still around, but the ink stain has been chipped away over the centuries by souvenir hunters, so it is now mostly a hole in the plaster.

Wartburg Castle has been referred to as one of the best preserved castles in Germany and a symbolic one. The castle was built in 1067 by a Count (Landgrave) Ludwig of Thuringia. Much of the early Romanesque portions of the castle palace remain, making it one of the few palaces of that period extant in Germany. The castle was restored with great attention to detail and added to with romantic revival elements in the 19th Century by architect Hugo von Ridgen. A detailed book of plans and progress of the restoration of Wartburg Castle can be found at the Castles Institute in Schloss Philippsburg over along on the Rhine. The book is also in the museum of Wartburg, but behind glass.

Wartburg Castle has a significance that goes much beyond its Luther history connection. Adolph Hitler considered it one of the "most German of castles" and the local town authorities had to battle with him, like Luther with his devil, when Wagnerian enthusiast Hitler wanted to replace the castle's Christian cross with a Swastika. One of the most impressive rooms within the castle is the Singers Hall (Sängersaal) or Hall of Minstrels, immortalized by Richard Wagner's opera "Tannhäuser", where in the middle ages, a contest of poets and minstrels was regularly held at Wartburg castle. Wagner took some poetic license of his own and set the action of the second act of his opera here. Wartburg and its Wagnerian Germanic identity also inspired "Mad" King Ludwig of Bavaria when he decided he needed a mountain top castle of his own.

In curious antithesis to its connection to Lutheran Protestantism, Wartburg Castle was also the home of a Roman Catholic Saint - Elizabeth of Hungary who was brought to Wartburg at the age of 4 and became the consort of Thuringian Count Ludwig IV. After his death, she became devoted to charity and was responsible for enough miracles to be canonized after her own early death, and made Saint Elizabeth. Her chambers at the castle are one of the focuses of a tour through the Romanesque palace where the rooms are mostly devoid of furniture, with the wonderful medieval art motifs of the walls remaining the only reminder of the grandeur of the times. One of the striking wall paintings is of the burial procession of the death of St. Elizabeth.

While Eisnenach was a symbol of German unification in the 1800s for its gathering of protesting students in 1817, demanding the unifying of disparate fiefdoms into a modern German nation, the Burschenschaften, the town and its famous castle rather suffered the worse for the division of Germany into east and west after WWII. The castle's once great armor collection was looted by the Russians and its furnishings vanished under East German control. A few pieces remain in the museum. The city of Eisenach itself became an industrial town during the East German years,

known for the manufacture of an East German car named for it. Today, Eisenach still retains some of its industrial feel, but the old town center has a square of historic half-wood buildings and stone medieval period gate house remaining from the city walls.

The Castle of Wartburg sits high on a mountain cliff above the town with great views of the forested countryside, some of the most beautiful woods in Germany. Wartburg castle was designated as a UNESCO World Heritage site in 1999 and is a very popular tourist destination for its historic and religious importance. It can get very crowded on weekends or summer holiday periods. A guided tour is required to see inside the old palace and museum, but part of the grounds and courtyard can be wandered without paid admission. Luther's Room is after the tour and climbing the winding wooden staircase of the medieval south tower affords a view of the castle and the surrounding forests.

There is a restaurant at Wartburg Castle with a terrace view for a snack or lunch, or if you don't feel like sitting, when heading back to the car or town, stop for a real Thuringia sausage. There is a car park near the castle, which can be filled at busy times. Busses line up underneath the walking bridge to the castle gates. From the city without a car the castle can be reached by a half-hour marked walk up the wooded hill or by city bus from the train station.

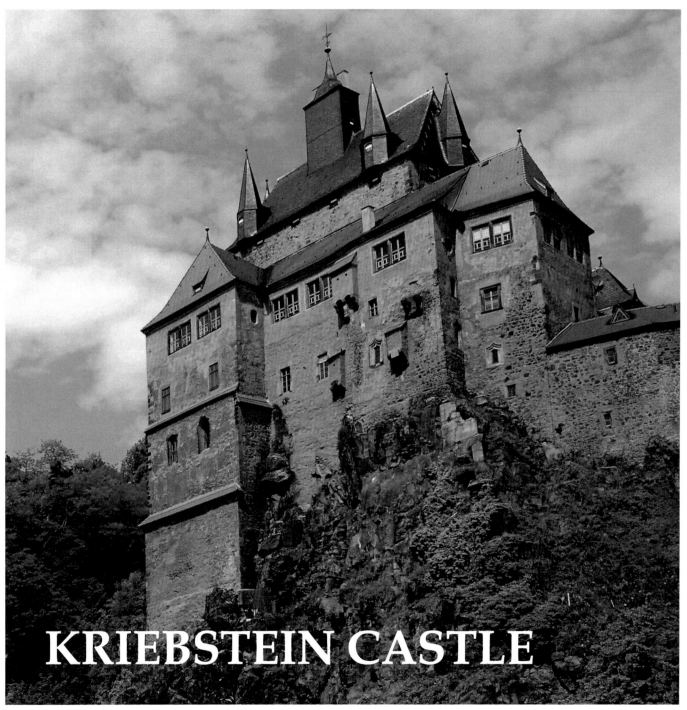

KRIEBSTEIN CASTLE

Knights Castle of Waldheim Saxony

Kriebstein Castle stands dramatically on a steep rock cliff over the Zschopau River, just two miles upstream from Waldheim, sometimes called Saxony's most beautiful "Knights Castle". It stands on the outer stone edge of a foothill where the river flows around on three sides in a deep ravine, providing an excellent defensive position, with entrance from a former drawbridge across a deep dry moat on the hill-facing side, surrounded by thick forested woods. The castle's form is a combined tower keep and ring fortress design. The residential tower rises from the sharp rock cliff above the river, giving the castle its dramatic face, while the oval ring encompasses the kitchens, a utility building, the chapel and tower gate house. At the heart of the complex is the vaulted gothic hall. The banquet hall in the extended wing is used as the concert and performance venue.

Kriebstein Castle was built beginning in 1384 by Dietrich von Beerwalde as a residence and ruling seat for his family estate which included the towns of Waldheim and Hartha, with the original castle completed by 1407, only a year before his death when Dietrich's widow Elizabeth inherited the castle and lands. In 1465, the Kriebstein castle and estate was acquired by Hugold III von Schleinitz, Lord Marshal to the Elector Ernest and Duke Albert, the Wettin rulers of Saxony. Schleinitz began an expansion of the fortress in 1471, commissioned from the master architect of Meissen's Albrectsburg Castle, Arnold von Westfallen. This period gave the castle most of its current shape with the construction of the utility wing, adding the Gothic Ballroom and Well Chamber, as well as the kitchens with his signature window designs. Later extensions and some structural additions from this period of the castle's 15th Century character remain intact.

After Hugold von Schleinitz's death in 1490, ownership changed hands a number of times preventing further additions, though the Kriebstein territory reached its most expansive importance by 1550 under Georg von Carlowitz. The late 1600s saw some renovations under the rulers of Schoenberg with floors connecting the residential tower and gatehouse. Some modest additions of the Lords von Milkau are commemorated by an inscription on the weather vanes. The castle was finally acquired by Hanscarl von Arnim of the House of Planitz near Zwickau in 1825 and the property remained in the hands of the Arnim family until the division of Germany at the end of World War II in 1945. The Arnim's made a number of alterations in Neo-Gothic style between 1866 and 1868 under the supervision of Saxony Court Master Builder Carl Moritz Haenelm, with some significant structural changes to the residence and defensive walls, but maintaining the essential medieval character of the castle. Since 1993, Kriebstein Castle and its museum have been owned by the Free State of Saxony.

Legend of the Faithful Lady of Kriebstein. A principal medieval legend of Kriebstein dates from the stormy period after the end of the Von Beerwalde dynasty. In 1415, a knight named Dietrich von Staupitz and his men at arms took the castle in a surprise assault. The

Saxony Margrave Frederick the Belligerent laid siege to the castle for the unauthorized land grab. After a long desperate time under siege, von Staupitz's wife begged of the count that he allow the women to leave the castle with the most "precious belongings they could carry". Frederick expected them to be holding their jewels and finery, but when he granted permission, was stunned when the castle gate was opened and the women were carrying their husbands on their backs. The lord was so touched by the clever deception of the faithful ladies of Kriebstein that he pardoned the greedy knight.

For visitors today the Castle Kriebstein hosts a number of events through the year with medieval reenactments, knight's battles, music concerts and holiday festivals. There is a small children's toy museum in the castle and an armory collection. The castle inn restaurant the "Zum Hungerturm" named for the intersection of the tower and the wall known in local terms as the "Starving Dungeon" has seating for 36 indoors and 24 in the garden for lunch or afternoon tea.

Open hours are Tuesday to Sunday 10 am – 4 pm February 15th through March. 10 am to 5:30 pm April to October and Saturday / Sunday / Holidays in November. Closed Mondays and in December and January. Last admission is an hour before closing. Kriebstein Castle is included with a Schloesserland Pass for free admission to permanent exhibits and reduced admission to special exhibitions. Kriebstein Castle is about 30 minutes from Leipzig or Dresden on the route A14. There is limited parking near the castle with a large car park at the Water Dam with a 15 minute walk up a marked footpath.

ROCHLITZ CASTLE

Elizabeth Von Rochlitz and the Reformation

Rochlitz Castle is one of the most important of the medieval castles associated with the Wettin family dynasty which ruled the Saxony regions of Germany and parts of Poland, with branches leading to the Imperial Throne of the Holy Roman German kings and Austrian Empire, and to the English throne of the Windsors, through Queen Victoria's husband Prince Albert of Saxe-Coburg. The castle is most associated with Elisabeth Von Rochlitz, who was the first to introduce Martin Luther's Reformation in Saxony against the virulent objections of her father-in-law, George "the Bearded" Duke of Saxony. The "of Rochlitz" is more a nickname for her residence at the castle following the death of her husband, as she was more officially Elisabeth Countess of Hesse and Duchess of Saxony. She came from Marburg in Hesse to marry Prince John of Saxony, but found her relations in Dresden difficult as a convert to Lutheranism. When her husband died in 1537, she was granted Rochlitz and Kriebstein as part of her "Wittum" a widow's dowery, and declared her lands to be Protestant. But Elisabeth only lived in Rochlitz Castle for ten years before returning to Hesse in 1547, gaining the lands of Hessian Schmalkalden. It was another Wettin, Frederick III of Saxony who hid Martin Luther at Wartburg Castle following the Edict of Worms, where he began his bible translation.

The castle at Rochlitz is over a thousand years old, built in early form in the 10th Century. The first documented record of the fortress is from 1009, when the Margrave named Gunselin, in an inheritance dispute with his nephews, rather un-like King Lear, had the castle burned down, rather than divide it. In 1143, the Margrave Konrad I of Wettin acquired the lands and in the following centuries the castle of Rochlitz rose in importance with the power of the Wettins of Saxony. As early as 1156, the castle was joined in a rapid expansion of colonial holdings under Konrad's fourth son, Dedo.

Rochlitz Castle became the permanent residence of Margrave Wilhelm the First at the end of the 14th Century. He was the count who turned the defensive fortress into a residence palace castle, giving it much of its current form. Further refurbishments were made at the end of the 15th Century under the Wettins, who divided the branches of the family

between Ernest and Albert, as a widow's resident seat for their sister Amalia, before the widow's dower tradition was transferred to the most famous resident Duchess Elisabeth in 1537. Following Elisabeth's return to Hesse, the castle and lands fell to the Saxony Elector Christian I and his wife Sophie, who had the medieval Rochlitz castle converted to a hunting lodge castle, preferring the newer Baroque palaces of Meissen and Dresden as residences. During the Thirty Years War the castle was besieged a number of times. In the

19th Century it was turned into a court and a jail, and at the end of WWII served as an allied detention camp for German military officers. During the East Germany communist days, the castle was an administrative office. Since April of 2013 the castle's residential living and state apartments have been opened to visitors.

A self-guided tour leads through a labyrinthine connection of halls and stairs around the outer chambers. The most distinctive feature of the castle are the twin towers rising above the banks of the Zwickau Mulde River, which give it more the appearance of a cathedral than a fortress. The towers are named "Light Jupe" and "Dark Jupe", but where a church might have a bell, the towers housed two dungeons. The towers were originally designed for residence chambers, but were never finished as living quarters. In one tower 142 steps to the top allow panoramic views of the city

of Rochlitz and the Mulde Valley. On the way up, the steps pass the jail cells, with one of them a recreated torture chamber. The other tower houses a library not open to the public.

The Prince's House and Transept offer access to the restored Prince's Parlor and the Feast Hall. One of the more unique architectural elements is the castle chapel with its Gothic ribbed vaulted ceiling. The

medieval chapel was one of the restorations ordered by the Wettins for their dowager sister Duchess Amalia of Saxony, with the redesign by imperial architect Arnold of Westphalia. Amalia further had the walls painted with frescos, with some of the original fragments of the painting still visible.

The preserved and recreated medieval castle kitchen, takes up a large area on the lower floor, dominated by a broad fireplace hearth and chimney. Once bustling with activity the aromas from the kitchen would have spread through the whole castle and its common name "the Black Kitchen" comes from the soot on the walls and ceiling remaining from the middle ages. In the cellar, partly hewn from the solid rock and brick, the "Long Cellar" was used as a panty for its cool temperatures, and the ceiling shows the imprints of the boarding from the medieval construction. The West Wall Walk leads from one of the towers to the back defensive entrance of the castle and another walk connects with the Prince's House residential rooms where you can still see some of the cannon ball damage left from the 30 Years War of Succession, the religion infused contest between Protestant and Catholic rulers of Europe.

Rochlitz Castle is about 30 minutes from Leipzig and 40 minutes from Dresden. The castle is open Tuesday to Sunday and legal holidays 10 am to 6 pm from March to October, closed November to February. Last Admission is 5 pm. Rochlitz Caste in included in the Sachsen Schloesserland Pass, with the castle free and discounted special exhibits, if you intent to visit some of the many other castles, gardens and palaces of Saxony.

CASTLE RÖTTELN

Autumn Castle in Baden-Württemberg

The casual traveler to Europe is unlikely to come across Burg Rötteln unless an avid castle hunter, touring Germany's Black Forest or visiting Basel, Switzerland. This wonderful castle ruin is at the southern end of Germany's Black Forest region, near the town of Lorrach. It is also in reach of a visit to Strasbourg and the Alsace Wine Road or Mulhouse. This early 13th Century castle was first documented as a completed fortress in 1259, but its first family namesake Walter von Rötteln was mentioned as participating in the tournament in Magdeburg as far back as 938. It is located in the most southwest corner of Germany where Germany touches Switzerland and France, with some of the country's most sunny

climates, and is one of the largest castle complexes in southern Baden-Württemburg.

After having spent much of a trip in southern Germany in the fog and overcast of fall, it was in this corner that the sun first shone on these well preserved ruins in the autumn leaves that inspired an enthusiastic photo taking still in film days. Some of the unique features of the castle

are: a still intact drawbridge crossing and portico; a "donjon" square tower which rises prominently over the landscape, and very clearly defined walls of original construction providing a beautiful example of inner and outer bailey medieval castle architecture more associated with France and England than other German castles. The castle resides on a sloping wooded hill where the defensive loop ports give a clear view of any advancing attackers. And although much of the inner walls have been destroyed, the defensive battlement walkways along the high walls have been restored, providing an almost dizzying vantage point overlooking the whole structure, but not sufficient to save it from French cannons in the War of Succession in 1678.

The castle is open all year 'round with a small museum of armor and other artifacts. The city of Lorrach holds an annual theater festival of performances at the castle from June to August. The castle of Burg Rötteln can be reached off the A5 and Route 317 between Basel and Neustadt, where very popular skiing areas are located in winter and not far from one of the great medieval castles of France, the Chateau Haut Koenigsbourg in the Alsace region on the other side of the upper Rhine valley.

83

AUF SCHÖNBURG

RHINE CASTLE HOTEL

Medieval Walls and Wine in Oberwesel On the Rhine

Ancient Germanic and Nordic legends tell of a dwarf, so enamored of the gold shining in the rocks through the shimmering waters of the Rhine River that he steals it from its guardians, the Rhine maidens, forges it into a ring which ultimately brings down the reign of the great Norse gods, with the ascension of man. The myth of the Rheingold inspired Wagner to write his famed operas and J. R. R. Tolkien to pen his fantasy version of the "Lord of the Rings" begetting the popular Hollywood movies. If the legend were true, it would have happened in the bends of the Rhine River near the mighty Loreley rock, where one of the maidens would sing and cause sailors to wreck on the shoals. It is here, in the heart of what has been named as a UNESCO World Heritage site of the Middle Rhine, with castles crowning the banks of the river at nearly every bend that Rheingoldstrasse weaves along the hills above the river, a favorite of cyclists.

Oberwesel on the Rhine is a quaint and narrow little village ringed by medieval walls with ancient stone towers still intact, pressed between the river and the steep slopes of the hill banks where it makes a sharp bend just south of the infamous Loreley rock. A castle called Schönburg (beautiful castle) has been standing watch over Oberwesel for a thousand years. Since the 12th Century, the Dukes of Schönburg

ruled the lands and town of Oberwesel with the right to levy customs taxes on goods traversing the river and the old Roman road through the mountains. The medieval Schönburg castle, like many of the castles in the Rhineland-Palatine was burnt by the French in the Thirty Years War of Palatine Succession in 1689.

Schönburg Castle is now a hotel, rebuilt in the 19th Century during the Rhine's romantic revival and is one of Germany's most romantic lodging establishments, a true authentic castle hotel with its incredible view of the Rhine and the town below. The hotel has 2 single rooms and 18 double rooms with 2 luxury suites, furnished with four-poster beds and balconies facing the Rhine. The castle's common spaces are richly furnished in antiques, with its library offering a cozy hideaway seeming centuries past and a maze of hallways to explore. The castle's restaurant offers elegant dining with courtyard and terrace tables with picture perfect views of the river, though the weather along the Rhine can be as moody as a greedy bi-polar dwarf - "my precious". The Auf Schönburg Castle Hotel is well suited for exploring the wine vineyards and mountain trails of the Rhineland and the medieval Rhine towns of Rudesheim, St. Goar, Bacharach and Boppard.

The Burg Hotel and Restaurant Auf Schönburg can be reached by car along the Rhine River road from Bingen or Koblenz, or the fastest route through the hills from the A61 Autobahn exits 44 or 45. By train, the station at Oberwesel is about a mile from the hotel with a steep climb up the hill - if one wants the exercise, or take a taxi. Oberwesel is also a stop on the K-D Rhine Cruise line route and Oberwesel is the closest Rhine River town to the Frankfurt-Hahn airport served by Ryanair and other discount airlines, about 35 minutes by car, while Frankfurt-Main Airport is about an hour by car or rail.

While in Oberwesel, stroll to the far end of the town to see the medieval walls with 16 towers from the 13th Century, some of Germany's best preserved and still protecting from marauders above, and the beautiful St Martins Church on a bluff above the Rhine Valley, or the Gothic red Liebfrauenkirche just below the castle. Every other year at Oberwesel the town is taken over in spring at whitsun (Pentacost Sunday) by the "Medieval Spectaculum" a middle-ages style fair returning the old lost mythical days to the banks of the Rhine.

CASTLE THURANT

Guarding The Mosel Vineyards

Thurant Castle, standing on a vine-covered steep slope above the Mosel (Moselle) River where it is flat and wide between Coblenz and Cochem, above the town of Alken, has endured murder, the intrigues of succession, division by a wall and allied bombs. The older parts of the castle are ruins, but sections have remained and slowly recovered. The first construction of the castle was begun in 1197 under the Palatine Duke of Braunschweig. Castle Thurant gets its name from the fortified town of Thuron in today's Syria, unsuccessfully besieged by its builder in the Crusades under Frederick Barbarossa. Thurant resisted claims of the Hohenstaufens until being taken by the Archbishop of Cologne, Engelbert in 1216. Englebert was murdered after only nine years in control.

Perhaps the Thurant castle's most interesting history is after its transfer to the Wittelsbachs. Through parts of its existence Thurant has been divided, unlike Solomon's baby. After its fall under a siege in 1248, following a two year war with the city of Trier by its then occupant, the knight known as "Zorno", the ownership of the castle was actually divided between two Bishoprics. One half of Thurant was given to Coblenz and the other to Trier. The castle today is noted for its two towers at either end.

When the castle was divided between the two districts a wall was built between the two halves so each owner would have a defense. The towers are now called the Trier Tower and the Cologne Tower. Several families had claim to the castle over the years, until it was abandoned as a fortress in 1600s and remained a ruin until privately purchased in 1911. It suffered further damage in 1945 at the end of the Second World War as the allies where advancing toward the Rhine. Even today, it is privately owned by two families.

The current owners have been rebuilding and restoring the remaining features of the castle since the 1920s. Noted elements of the structure are its two high towers, defensive walkways, the current rebuilt manor house, the dividing wall, a castle chapel with an ornate Baroque altar and a rebuilt hunting lodge with displays of armor and hunting trophies.

Thurant Castle can clearly be seen from the river and the river route road (B49) and is easily reached up a road from the village of Alken on the south bank of the Mosel. There is a car parking area just below the wooden draw walkway to the castle gate with its spiked portcullis. There is a small refreshment bar inside. Castle Thurant is about 20 minutes from Cochem and 30 Minutes from Coblenz. It can also be reached via a shortcut from the Rhine River at Boppard via the (narrow) country road through Pfaffenheck.

TRAUSNITZ CASTLE

Wittelsbach Fortress in Landshut Bavaria

The Wittelsbachs were the ruling family of Bavaria. The Ludwigs and Maximillians whose palaces can be found all around Munich and environs, from the royal jewels at the Residence to the summer palaces at Schliessheim and Nymphenburg from the Baroque period, even to the faux Disney inspiration 19th Century gothic revival castle of Neuschwanstein, but few actual medieval fortress castles (burgs) survive of the Bavarian royals. One of the most significant sits atop a hill over-looking the town of Landshut on the Isar River, about 40 minutes to the north east of Munich.

Trausnitz Castle is the ancestral home of the Wittelsbach Dukes of Lower Bavaria, called in their day the "Rich Dukes" of Bavaria-Landshut. The Town of Landshut was founded in 1204 by Duke Ludwig I. The castle in its medieval present fortress form with an almost intact ring of fortifications with peel towers, battlements and gates, mostly from the late 1400s, presents impressive German style medieval architecture. The high square keep known as the Wittelsbach Tower at the foremost edge of the promontory is the most distinctive feature of Trausnitz Castle from outside the walls.

Inside the courtyard, one sees the later Renaissance palace additions with a more Italianate feel of stacked arch walks and layered stairways. A tour of the castle features the vaulted Gothic Old Knights Hall, the St. George Chapel with unique winged alter sculptures and the statue of St. George slaying the dragon. The wood paneled chambers represent the castle's time as a Renaissance period residence in the 16th Century with the famous Fool's Staircase depicting fresco scenes of the Italian Commedia dell'arte. The tour ends with a view of the town and surrounding countryside from the balcony. Burg Trausnitz remained in its medieval state when Duke Ludwig V built his palace residence in the town below in 1536.

The Wittelsbachs were avid collectors of art and curios. The Kunst and Wunderkammer Museum at Burg Trausnitz Castle founded by Duke Albrecht in 1565 was one of the precursors of today's modern museums, born of the Renaissance of the 16th Century when art and the natural wonders of the world took on a mutual significance of the opening of knowledge and curiosity beyond the religious dogma of the dark ages. The Art and Wonder Chamber, divided into the categories of Artificialia, Naturalia, Exotica and Scientifica holds a fascinating collection of exotic art from far flung lands, curiosity specimens of nature, early scientific instruments of astrolabes and

automates, and intriguing art works of sculpture, rock crystal cups and cabinets of amber, as well as portraits of the assorted Wittelsbachs.

The castle tour takes about 45 minutes and the museum can be visited separately without taking the tour. The Burgshrank café offers snacks on a terrace overlooking the west approach. Opening times are 9 am to 6 pm daily April through September and 10 am to 4 pm October through March. Last admission is 30 minutes before closing. Trausnitz Castle can be reached by train to Landshut and #7 city bus to the Kalcherstrasse stop, by car. Landshut is just off the A92 autobahn, about 15 minutes from the Munich International Airport, requiring a winding drive up to the castle parking lot the from city's main road. The castle itself is about a 7-10 minute walk from parking lot through the Hofgarten Green Park. The castle can also be reached by a steep hike from the town below.

Four times a year, twice in summer, the town of Landshut re-enacts the "Landshut Wedding" celebrating the marriage of Georg, the son of Duke Ludwig "the Rich" to Hedwig, the daughter of the King of Poland in 1475. The celebrations are in the town center surrounding the gothic cathedral and a recreated medieval village in the town fair grounds below the castle. Landshut also celebrates Carnival in February and Strong Beer Festival in March as well as a Christkindle Christmas Market.

Made in United States
North Haven, CT
11 February 2024

48647849R00058